C000176159

by Iain Gray

Lang**Syne**

PUBLISHING

WRITING *to* REMEMBER

Lang**Syne**

PUBLISHING

WRITING *to* REMEMBER

79 Main Street, Newtongrange,
Midlothian EH22 4NA
Tel: 0131 344 0414   Fax: 0845 075 6085
E-mail: info@lang-syne.co.uk
www.langsyneshop.co.uk

Design by Dorothy Meikle
Printed by Ricoh Print Scotland
© Lang Syne Publishers Ltd 2015

ISBN 978-1-85217-209-1

Millar

MOTTO:

The Best Things await Us in Heaven.

*Echoes of a far distant past
can still be found in most names*

Chapter one:

Origins of Scottish surnames

by George Forbes

It all began with the Normans.

For it was they who introduced surnames into common usage more than a thousand years ago, initially based on the title of their estates, local villages and chateaux in France to distinguish and identify these landholdings, usually acquired at the point of a bloodstained sword.

Such grand descriptions also helped enhance the prestige of these arrogant warlords and generally glorify their lofty positions high above the humble serfs slaving away below in the pecking order who only had single names, often with Biblical connotations as in Pierre and Jacques.

The only descriptive distinctions among this peasantry concerned their occupations, like Pierre the swineherd or Jacques the ferryman.

The Normans themselves were originally Vikings (or Northmen) who raided, colonised and eventually settled down around the French coastline.

They had sailed up the Seine in their long-boats in 900AD under their ferocious leader Rollo and ruled the roost in north east France before sailing over to conquer England, bringing their relatively new tradition of having surnames with them.

It took another hundred years for the Normans to percolate northwards and surnames did not begin to appear in Scotland until the thirteenth century.

These adventurous knights brought an aura of chivalry with them and it was said no damsel of any distinction would marry a man unless he had at least two names.

The family names included that of Scotland's great hero Robert De Brus and his compatriots were warriors from families like the De Morevils, De Umphravils, De Berkelais, De Quincis, De Viponts and De Vaux.

As the knights settled the boundaries of

their vast estates, they took territorial names, as in Hamilton, Moray, Crawford, Cunningham, Dunbar, Ross, Wemyss, Dundas, Galloway, Renfrew, Greenhill, Hazelwood, Sandylands and Church-hill.

Other names, though not with any obvious geographical or topographical features, nevertheless derived from ancient parishes like Douglas, Forbes, Dalyell and Guthrie.

Other surnames were coined in connection with occupations, castles or legendary deeds. Stuart originated in the word steward, a prestigious post which was an integral part of any large medieval household. The same applied to Cooks, Chamberlains, Constables and Porters.

Borders towns and forts – needed in areas like the Debateable Lands which were constantly fought over by feuding local families – had their own distinctive names; and it was often from them that the resident groups took their communal titles, as in the Grahams of Annandale, the Elliots and Armstrongs of the East Marches, the Scotts and Kerrs of Teviotdale and Eskdale.

Even physical attributes crept into surnames, as in Small, Little and More (the latter being 'beg' in Gaelic), Long or Lang, Stark, Stout, Strong or Strang and even Jolly.

Mieklejohns would have had the strength of several men, while Littlejohn was named after the legendary sidekick of Robin Hood.

Colours got into the act with Black, White, Grey, Brown and Green (Red developed into Reid, Ruddy or Ruddiman). Blue was rare and nobody ever wanted to be associated with yellow.

Pompous worthies took the name Wiseman, Goodman and Goodall.

Words intimating the sons of leading figures were soon affiliated into the language as in Johnson, Adamson, Richardson and Thomson, while the Norman equivalent of Fitz (from the French-Latin 'filius' meaning 'son') cropped up in Fitzmaurice and Fitzgerald.

The prefix 'Mac' was 'son of' in Gaelic and clans often originated with occupations – as in MacNab being sons of the Abbot, MacPherson and MacVicar being sons of the minister and MacIntosh being sons of the chief.

The church's influence could be found in the names Kirk, Clerk, Clarke, Bishop, Friar and Monk. Proctor came from a church official, Singer and Sangster from choristers, Gilchrist and Gillies from Christ's servant, Mitchell, Gilmory and Gilmour from servants of St Michael and Mary, Malcolm from a servant of Columba and Gillespie from a bishop's servant.

The rudimentary medical profession was represented by Barber (a trade which also once included dentistry and surgery) as well as Leech or Leitch.

Businessmen produced Merchants, Mercers, Monypennies, Chapmans, Sellers and Scales, while down at the old village watermill the names that cropped up included Miller, Walker and Fuller.

Other self explanatory trades included Coopers, Brands, Barkers, Tanners, Skinners, Brewsters and Brewers, Tailors, Saddlers, Wrights, Cartwrights, Smiths, Harpers, Joiners, Sawyers, Masons and Plumbers.

Even the scenery was utilised as in Craig, Moor, Hill, Glen, Wood and Forrest.

Rank, whether high or low, took its place with Laird, Barron, Knight, Tennant, Farmer, Husband, Granger, Grieve, Shepherd, Shearer and Fletcher.

The hunt and the chase supplied Hunter, Falconer, Fowler, Fox, Forrester, Archer and Spearman.

The renowned medieval historian Froissart, who eulogised about the romantic deeds of chivalry (and who condemned Scotland as being a poverty stricken wasteland), once sniffily dismissed the peasantry of his native France as the jacquerie (or the jacques-without-names) but it was these same humble folk who ended up over-throwing the arrogant aristocracy.

In the olden days, only the blueblooded knights of antiquity were entitled to full, proper names, both Christian and surnames, but with the passing of time and a more egalitarian, less feudal atmosphere, more respectful and worthy titles spread throughout the populace as a whole.

Echoes of a far distant past can still be found in most names and they can be borne with pride in commemoration of past generations who fought and toiled in some capacity or other to make our nation what it now is, for good or ill.

Chapter two:

For freedom's cause

Originally an occupational surname denoting those who were engaged in the important tasks of not only the milling of cereals but also the treatment of flax and the finishing of cloth, Millar is now one of the most common surnames found in the English-speaking world.

There is nothing common, however, about the generations of Millars who left an indelible mark on the rich tapestry of Scotland's story or who have achieved international celebrity and fame.

Millar, with a 'a', is the most common spelling of the name found in Scotland, and other variations, apart from Miller, with an 'e', have included Mylar, Myler and Millare, while the Latin form of Molindarius is found in Scotland as early as the thirteenth century.

This Latin form survives today in the name of the Molendinar burn, or stream, which is said to wind its way under the streets of present-day Glasgow city centre after flowing under the historic cathedral.

One enduring myth is that the beer brewed by a famous Glasgow brewery that once took its waters from the Molendinar was 'blessed by the bones of St. Mungo', because the stream flowed over the earthly remains of the city's patron saint!

Still on a religious theme, but much further south in the county of Dumfriesshire, a family of Mylers who were settled there for centuries had their own confident motto of 'The best things await us in heaven.'

Those skilled in the art of milling were to be found in practically every Scottish community, including the diverse community of clans of the Highlands and Islands.

Some Millars of today, albeit with a great deal of genealogical effort, could possibly trace a descent from these clans but it is to one clan in particular, the proud MacFarlanes, that the links are particularly strong.

Millars who can trace a descent from the MacFarlane ancestral homelands of Arrochar, on the shores of Loch Long on the western mainland, are regarded as a sept, or branch, of the clan, and are entitled to share in its rich heritage and traditions.

As kinsfolk of the MacFarlanes the Millars shared in both the fortunes and misfortunes of this clan whose motto is 'This I'll defend' and whose crest is a savage brandishing a sword and pointing with his left hand to a crown.

This clan with which the Millars were inextricably linked descends from an Earl of Lennox whose younger son, Gilchrist, received the Arrochar lands towards the end of the twelfth century.

The clan name stems from the Gaelic MacPharlain, meaning 'son of Parlan', who was a grandson of Gilchrist of Arrochar.

The MacFarlanes, along with their kinsfolk such as the Millars, were firm in their defence of Scotland's freedom during the bitter and bloody Wars of Independence with England.

They not only fought at the side of the great warrior king Robert the Bruce at the battle of Bannockburn, but also provided him with help in one of his desperate hours of need.

Bruce, who had been enthroned as King of Scots at Scone in March of 1306, was defeated less than three months later at the battle of Methven, near Perth.

Fleeing with a small band of fellow survivors, they found themselves in the lands of the Earl of Lennox who, recognising the sound of his king's hunting horn, offered them much needed rest and refreshment before Bruce made his way to Dunaverty, on the tip of the Kintyre peninsula, and from there to sanctuary on the island of Rathlin.

It had been to Duncan MacFarlane of Arrochar's encampment that the earl had led Bruce and his men, while Duncan and a contingent of MacFarlanes fought under the command of the earl at Bannockburn in June of 1314, when a 20,000-strong English army under Edward II was defeated by a Scots army less than half this strength.

Ironically, it was through a misguided sense of chivalry that the battle occurred in the first place.

By midsummer of 1313 the mighty fortress of Stirling Castle was occupied by an English garrison under the command of Sir Philip Mowbray.

Bruce's hotheaded brother, Edward, agreed to a pledge by Mowbray that if the castle was not relieved by battle by midsummer of the following year, then he would surrender.

This made battle inevitable, and by June 23 of 1314 the two armies faced one another at Bannockburn, in sight of the castle.

It was on this day that Bruce slew the English knight Sir Henry de Bohun in single combat, but the battle proper was not fought until the following day, shortly after the rise of the midsummer sun.

The English cavalry launched a desperate but futile charge on the densely packed ranks of Scottish spearmen known as schiltrons, and by the time the sun had sank slowly in the west the

English army had been totally routed, with Edward himself only narrowly managing to make his escape from the carnage of the battlefield.

Scotland's independence had been secured, to the glory of Bruce and his loyal army and at terrible cost to the English.

The roles were reversed in 1513, however, when up to 5000 Scots, including James IV, an archbishop, two bishops, eleven earls, fifteen barons, and 300 knights were slain at the battle of Flodden after the monarch had crossed the border into England.

Included in the ranks of the Scots were about 7,500 clansmen, including Sir Iain MacFarlane, son of the 10th Chief of Clan MacFarlane, who fell along with his clansmen and kinsmen such as the Millars.

Nearly thirty-five years later, in 1547, Sir Iain's grandson, the 13th chief of the clan, was among the Scots killed at the battle of Pinkie, near Musselburgh, on Scotland's east coast, while attempting to repel an English invasion under the command of the Duke of Somerset.

Sir Iain had been among the 3,000 clansmen who had fought under the Earl of Argyll.

A dispute over the rights to the earldom of Lennox would appear to have been the reason why the MacFarlanes later found themselves in opposition to the ill-starred Mary, Queen of Scots, whose second husband, Lord Darnley, had been recognised as heir to the earldom.

Mary's final defeat by the forces that had coerced her into abdicating in favour of her infant son, James, came at the battle of Langside, fought on the southern outskirts of Glasgow on May 13, 1568.

Following her escape from Lochleven Castle, Mary and a force of loyal supporters had been en route from Hamilton to the bastion of Dumbarton Castle when they met the forces of her half-brother the Earl of Moray, who was the Regent, at Langside.

The Queen's army, commanded by the

Earl of Argyll, suffered a disastrous defeat and Andrew MacFarlane, 14th chief of the clan, is said to have captured three of the royal standards.

One account of the vital role that he and his clansmen and kinsmen played in the battle states how 'in the hottest of the fight he came up with 300 of his friends and countrymen and, falling fiercely on the flank of the queen's army, then threw them into irretrievable disorder, and this mainly contributed to decide the fortune of the day.'

A grateful Regent is said to have rewarded the clan after the battle with its present crest and motto.

Chapter three:

Thieves and Jacobites

**The MacFarlanes and their Millar kinsmen
appear to have had a spirited taste for adven-
ture and, when not fighting enemies in the
form of English invaders or deposed queens,
took delight in preying on their neighbours.**

This proved to have dire consequences
for the clan and their kinsfolk, however, when in
July of 1624 many of them were convicted of
theft and robbery, while in 1642 their nefarious
activities began to prove such a threat to law and
order that the clan was actually proscribed and
their lands forfeited under an Act of Estates.

Earlier, in 1594, they had been
denounced by the royal authority as 'being in
the habit of committing theft, robbery and
oppression.' Much of their cattle raiding took
place on nights of a full moon, to such an
extent that the moon itself came to be known
as 'MacFarlane's lantern'!

Under the 1642 Act, many deposed MacFarlanes and their kinsfolk such as the Millars found new homes in Aberdeenshire and Kincardineshire, where some adopted new names such as McInnes and Stewart.

Many other unruly clans suffered a similar fate to that of the MacFarlanes as an exasperated James VI attempted to impose the rule of law on his unruly subjects.

An example of his attitude towards his unruly subjects in the Highlands and Islands can be found in his statement that 'as for the Highlanders, I shortly comprehend them all in two sorts of people; the one that dwelleth in our mainland, that are barbarous for the most part, but are yet mixed with some civility: the other, that dwelleth in the isles, that are utterly barbarous, without any sort of show of civility.'

By the mid-eighteenth century Millars (in the numerous spelling variations of the name) were to be found in large groups all over Scotland, and the name frequently appears in the official Muster Roll of Prince Charles Edward Stuart's Army, 1745-46.

A Jacobite Rising in 1715 to restore the Royal House of Stuart to the throne had ended in failure, but thirty years later, in July of 1745, Prince Charles Edward Stuart, fondly remembered by Jacobites as 'Bonnie Prince Charlie' and derogatorily referred to by Hanoverians as 'The Young Pretender', arrived from France on the Hebridean island of Eriskay.

The Royal Standard was raised at Glenfinnan the following month, and numerous clans rallied to his cause.

Victory was achieved at the battle of Prestonpans in September, and in October the confident prince and his army set off on the long march south to London to claim what was believed to be the rightful Stuart inheritance of the throne.

The army reached only as far as Derby, however, before the controversial decision was taken in early December to withdraw back over the border.

On April 16, 1746, Jacobite hopes were dashed forever when the army was defeated by the Duke of Cumberland and his Hanoverian forces at the battle of Culloden, fought on Drummossie Moor, near Inverness.

The Jacobite muster roll records an Alexander Miller, who was a servant in the Atholl Brigade to Lord George Murray, the prince's lieutenant general, while James Millar was with a troop of cavalry that had been raised in Edinburgh after the victory at Prestonpans.

Seven Millars are listed as having served with the Forfarshire (Ogilvy's) Regiment, including David Millar, a shoemaker from Brechin, James Millar, a brewer from Coupar, and James Millar, a horse-hirer from Dundee.

Hugh Millar was with MacDonnell of Glengarry's Regiment, while another Millar served with MacPherson of Cluny's Regiment.

There is also a record of a James Miller in the Manchester Regiment, which had been raised during the army's march through England.

The slaughter meted out to the Jacobite

army at Culloden did not end with the battle itself, with victorious government troops embarking on an orgy of slaughter, rape and plunder for several terrible months.

The defeat not only put paid to the prospect of a Stuart restoration, but also sounded the death knell for an entire way of life that had existed for centuries in the Highlands and Islands with, for example, the carrying of arms, wearing of kilts, and playing of bagpipes banned by law.

This marked the start of the great migrations from the Highlands, with many clansmen and their kinsmen such as the Millars forced to seek a new life elsewhere – either in the Scottish Lowlands or on foreign shores.

Many of the name, whether spelt with an 'a' or an 'e', would subsequently gain acclaim in pursuits ranging from music and sport to literature and science.

Chapter four:

On the world stage

A feisty lady who was born in the Ayrshire coastal resort of Saltcoats in 1792 has the unusual distinction of being the first female captain of a British ship to be registered in the British Register of Tonnage.

As the master (or, perhaps more properly, the mistress) of the two-masted brig *The Clytus*, Captain Betsy Miller sailed with cargoes of coal from Saltcoats and Ardrossan to Dublin, returning with cargoes of limestone.

Her father, Captain William Miller, was a wood merchant and ship owner and it was following the death of his son in 1827 that he allowed his 35-year-old daughter to take his place as skipper of *The Clytus* and her fourteen-man crew.

The bold Betsy captained the vessel until her retiral in 1862, at the ripe old age of 70, and two years before her death.

A popular tourist destination near Cromarty, in Easter Ross, is the cottage where the self-taught stonemason and geologist Hugh Miller was born in 1802.

Fascinated by the fossils that he found near his home, he began an in-depth study of geology that resulted in a number of important books such as *Testimony of the Rocks* and *The Old Red Sandstone, Footprints of the Creator*.

In addition to his scientific studies, the intensely religious Miller also found time to help found the Free Church of Scotland, before his death in 1856.

On the field of battle, Duncan Millar was a 34-year-old private in the 42nd Regiment when he won the Victoria Cross, Britain's highest award for gallantry, for his actions during the Indian Mutiny in 1859.

With their officers killed during an attack at Maylah Gate, Millar and another private helped to direct the rest of their comrades in repelling the attackers, and his medal is now on display at the National War Museum of Scotland, at Edinburgh Castle.

Another winner of the Victoria Cross was James Millar, a 26-year-old private with the 7th Battalion of the King's Own (Royal Lancaster) Regiment during the bloody battle of the Somme in July of 1916.

Despite being mortally wounded while delivering a vital message, he not only managed to carry out his mission but also was able to return with an answer before falling dead at the feet of his officer.

In more contemporary times, and in the sporting arena, Ian Millar is the world show jumping champion who was born in Halifax, Nova Scotia, in 1947, while Robert Millar, born in 1958, is the Scottish professional cyclist who won the 'king of the mountains' competition and finished fourth in the 1984 Tour de France – the only time that a Briton has won one of the major tour classifications.

In the world of music, Glenn Miller was the popular bandleader, trombonist and composer who was born in the rural town of Clarinda, Iowa, in 1904. Dropping a college degree for a life in music, he played with a number of bands, culminating in his own band, the Glenn Miller Orchestra.

He was accepted into the U.S. Army in 1942 with the rank of captain and ordered to put his musical skills to use by 'putting a little more spring into the feet of our marching men and a little more joy into their hearts.'

Miller and his 50-strong orchestra did not disappoint: touring as the Glenn Miller Army Air Force Band, they played at military bases, factories and made radio broadcasts.

The band visited Britain in July of 1944, and on December 15th of that year Miller boarded a plane from England to Paris to finalise arrangements for a Christmas broadcast.

The aircraft mysteriously disappeared somewhere over the channel, and has never been found – fuelling a number of conspiracy theories that persist to this day as to the true circumstances surrounding the band leader's death.

Millars/Millers have also achieved celebrity as gifted writers, including the novelist Henry Miller, who was born in New York City in 1891 and died in 1980.

His best known works include *Tropic of Cancer, Tropic of Capricorn*, and *Black Spring*, and when *Tropic of Cancer* was published in America in 1961 it immediately led to a number of obscenity trials.

The U.S. Supreme Court, however, in a landmark decision, ruled that the book was not obscene but a work of literature.

Arthur Miller, the son of Jewish immigrants to America and who was born in New York in 1915, is remembered not only as a gifted playwright, but also as one of the husband's of the glamorous Hollywood star Marilyn Monroe.

He wrote his first play, *No Villain*, in 1936, while his 1949 play *Death of a Salesman* won a Pulitzer Prize, and three Tony awards. Another award winning play, *The Crucible*, opened on Broadway in 1953, three years before his marriage to Monroe and eight years before the couple's eventual divorce.

Miller, who died in February of 2005, was also a staunch advocate of freedom of speech and human rights, and was found guilty of contempt of Congress in 1957 for refusing to name members of a literary group who were suspected of harbouring Communist sympathies.

The conviction was overturned a year later by the U.S. Court of Appeals.

Another literary Millar, although perhaps not as highbrow as Arthur Miller and Henry Miller, was William Miller, known as 'The Laureate of the Nursery'.

Born in Glasgow in 1810, Miller, who died in 1872, worked as a wood-turner and cabinet-maker.

But he was also an accomplished poet and songwriter, and is particularly remembered today for the popular children's nursery rhyme *Wee Willie Winkie*.

Raising the standard at Glenfinnan